[swee'ving]

In French, *suivre* is to follow, to keep, to attend, to understand, to watch, to listen, to take, to be undergoing—depending on the context in which it is used. The addition of the English present participle *-ing* implies the present continuous, that something is happening exactly now, or is happening just before or after now, or may continue into the future.

FLORENCE UNIACKE

SUIVING

[swee'ving]

MA BIBLIOTHÈQUE

FLORENCE UNIACKE

SUIVING

THE METEORS, BOOK II

MA BIBLIOTHÈQUE, LONDON

 Published 2020

Printed by Printed World Publishing, Hastings, Great Britain

Set in Didot, Linotype Didot, and Bodoni Ornaments

ISBN 978-1-910055-71-7

Papers used are from well-managed forests and responsible sources

LONDON, 2020

mirrer

errer

errOr

CONTENTS

COME WHEN YOU'RE READY

unsouled is the grief of thou century,
a haze whose eye is only me
will to do. In fantasy *I-I* stop'd—
on a rampant misery
that you must admit
total change
may not solve.

Eternally more
one and only reality
an airless arena
a mind
where concrete joys
and brutality excite
an all you can

dupe.

(‘Read some Gramsci!’ he called.
‘Oi Black Flag Bam Bam, it wasn’t
Gramsci who said that.’ she replied,
through the -masks -flares -explosives
‘…it was Collobert, or Leopoldine, do
some research!’ And high she went on
knowledge. Ecco Om.
Meanwhile a comrade whispered,
(‘I have no face, let me hold you as I can
only now.’)

The next station is Hyde Park Corner
and we too have a troubled relationship
to reading,
when coming to books with conceit
moving over their roily hills,
treading such itinerant grass and décor

um, stay.

Still! Only I rake
against the true variable
Transformation—
a head colours the pitted horizon,
there is only me
and I demand, I delay, I halt the potential
potency of a turnaround for all
as anything can gallop ahead
and supercede recognition
but nothing is not I.

Reclose the only militant here
burning unseen vantage
reconnoitre, could be I mime
& do.

The disguarded husk of Yes rests there
among the chief phrase,
so familiar to Oedipus—is a close friend
is Yes, No, its savage critique
is Yes, No, Daddy,
Yes, No, we will always be underneath
your interjection.

Take me to a place
as it may be now
where I only enjoy
what is here

My wish is that I am intimate
with the Prime Minister
as I am intimate with the Lord—Who's
in agreement we lie, belonging—
as uneasy men
we play, & tip the piggy bank
on to the bed, praying—
Lord / you who
give value—
to our shared rightness.

& burrow und'r this moustache
in2 the mowths hoopla 'f bad decision

after the sun'd
ay each jowel
october harden'd

All Hail this Xst-ream
class Bar/k osh kosh
cub clobber mmmm
'Sweetie, tell them what you do?'
'Big Ted, Euston road'
Cap-ME-rese.

TO LANGUAGE

voir le vous or boire un jour
je serait et quoi los bras be ca envelope
vlope vla velo vite quanb con soit abette ta
tebe front
bure colle culle cloc
oug ole x soup soop
biz q'qisque eess cleer
clees lee m lit lang
suit I am suiving le
Lan god gauge gobieux
gub du gobo trango quil
tranquil

de-tongue. fun ic.ecandle wick
crowning f.light Fit.uck
emi-nine mornings
sweat syllabubs/ llabites bit
tankers mansawnOr
ViOl sham dormee
mili lit
tar ped

c\l\oud. y'orifice
moot mut mou/th
sorb. Thumb. fableau.
y.owl
beat. lelegs tickle
h.ull gr. gir.l
granular laughter in the aisle
p.alm

\

On. oo. oon. onite
uuonite. soap'ng moon-datory
datory lievre HaR
ssspEeeeeeeeeeeeeeeed
stream >> RA. ray. rain. REIN >
Quee roar roe steam
tum ete O/range bird lifting
who/a hoRse man-e parted
fingers stat/U/at/e
fly. FlEW
fui

Spill-eau l'posse ran.ge rang. eRANGEd
hot\wide\dry PLAIN – trunc
milli-plage, lag.os lilac woop leather
bl.

two chairs chaise chasse chassis cassis hussy
ass as in as in sin sin que cos cosco ococo
wax xaw saw soar sarl roar rar art ar ohno

Uh! bash wing
clip run win
ver-million wet
mill sever
mill head.

Run t'or sum
Run to the sun.

AND BACK

The may of the gail
the fright of the out-breath
the centred life.

The might of the gail
the fray of the breath
the centred life,
the gailing wind.

I am come over
am brought upon a deep and long need
to be alone
here where it is
you encounter not
and boat around the hell
that is required to
come on inside a
part your huge form
three pommes for two
and you, and you, and who?

The angels volt

hup

hup

hup

hup